MARTIN LUTHER KING JR.

in his own words

Gareth Stevens
Publishing

Please visit our website, www.garethstevens.com. For a free color catalog of all our high-quality books, call toll free 1-800-542-2595 or fax 1-877-542-2596.

Library of Congress Cataloging-in-Publication Data

Nagelhout, Ryan.
Martin Luther King Jr. in his own words / by Ryan Nagelhout.
  p. cm. — (Eyewitness to history)
Includes index.
ISBN 978-1-4339-9932-1 (pbk.)
ISBN 978-1-4824-3290-9 (6-pack)
ISBN 978-1-4824-0147-9 (library binding)
1. King, Martin Luther, — Jr., — 1929-1968 — Juvenile literature. 2. African Americans — Biography — Juvenile literature. 3. Civil rights workers — United States — Biography — Juvenile literature. I. Nagelhout, Ryan. II. Title.
E185.97.K5 N34 2014
323—dc23

First Edition

Published in 2014 by
Gareth Stevens Publishing
111 East 14th Street, Suite 349
New York, NY 10003

Copyright © 2014 Gareth Stevens Publishing

Designer: Katelyn E. Reynolds
Editor: Therese Shea

Photo credits: Cover, p. 1 (Martin) Michael Ochs Archives/Getty Images; cover, p. 1 (background image) AFP/Getty Images; cover, p. 1 (logo quill icon) Seamartini Graphics Media/Shutterstock.com; cover, p. 1 (logo stamp) YasnaTen/Shutterstock.com; cover, p. 1 (color grunge frame) DmitryPrudnichenko/Shutterstock.com; cover, pp. 1–32 (paper background) Nella/Shutterstock.com; cover, pp. 1–32 (decorative elements) Ozerina Anna/Shutterstock.com; pp. 1–32 (wood texture) Reinhold Leitner/Shutterstock.com; pp. 1–32 (open book background) Elena Schweitzer/Shutterstock.com; pp. 1–32 (bookmark) Robert Adrian Hillman/Shutterstock.com; p. 4 Dennis K. Johnson/Lonely Planet Images/Getty Images; p. 5 Hulton Archive/Getty Images; p. 7 CBS Photo Archive/Getty Images; pp. 9, 11, 14 Michael Ochs Archives/Getty Images; pp. 12–13, 19 Don Cravens/Time & Life Pictures/Getty Images; p. 15 Popperfoto/Getty Images; pp. 16–17 Shel Hershorn/Hulton Archives/Getty Images; p. 18 (signature) McSush/ Wikipedia.com; pp. 20, 23 AFP/Getty Images; p. 21 Bob Gomel/Time & Life Pictures/ Getty Images; pp. 24–25 Cecil Stoughton, White House Press Office (WHPO)/ Wikipedia.com; p. 27 Lynn Pelham/Time & Life Pictures/Getty Images; p. 28 Jewel Samad/AFP/Getty Images.

Printed in the United States of America

CPSIA compliance information: Batch #CW14GS: For further information contact Gareth Stevens, New York, New York at 1-800-542-2595.

CONTENTS

*Words in the glossary appear in **bold** type the first time they are used in the text.*

A BITTER *Reminder*

Martin Luther King Jr., the famous civil rights leader, was born on January 15, 1929. The first 12 years of his life were spent at his grandparents' home on Auburn Avenue in Atlanta, Georgia.

King grew up a few miles from Stone Mountain, during a time when a monument to **Confederate** war heroes was being carved into its north side. The South of King's youth was deeply divided between black

NAME CHANGE

Martin Luther King Jr. was born Michael King Jr., after his father. Martin's father was a Baptist minister heavily influenced by the teachings of Martin Luther, a German religious reformer. Shortly after a trip to Germany, King Sr. decided to be known as "Martin Luther." Michael King Jr.'s name was changed to "Martin Luther King Jr." in 1934.

Stone Mountain monument

and white. The mountain's carvings were a reminder of a time of slavery. King was seeking change when he referred to Stone Mountain on the steps of the Lincoln Memorial years later. He did much to alter the course of civil rights through the delivery of one of the most famous speeches in American history.

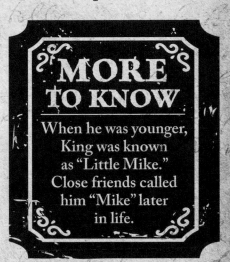

MORE TO KNOW

When he was younger, King was known as "Little Mike." Close friends called him "Mike" later in life.

Martin Luther King Jr. was a powerful public speaker. This skill—and his efforts in the civil rights movement—led to great changes in American society.

BROTHERS
and Sisters

JIM CROW LAWS

After the Thirteenth Amendment freed slaves in the United States, many states and cities passed laws to restrict the civil rights of blacks. Called Jim Crow laws, these measures made it hard for blacks to vote and segregated many areas of life. In Alabama, for example, blacks and whites weren't allowed to eat in the same restaurants or play pool together. Georgia even passed a law barring blacks and whites from being buried in the same cemetery.

The South was a very different place when Martin Luther King Jr. was growing up in Atlanta. Although slavery officially ended in 1865 with the Thirteenth Amendment, blacks didn't have the same rights as whites. **Segregation** kept whites and blacks separated with "whites only" businesses, parks, schools, and even drinking fountains.

King's religious beliefs helped him realize early in his life that segregation and Jim Crow laws weren't fair. In a sermon called "The Drum Major Instinct" delivered at Ebenezer Baptist Church in 1968, King said that *"all men are brothers because they are children of a common father."* He believed that all people came from God and thus they were equal and deserved to be treated as peers.

MORE TO KNOW

Jim Crow was a common name for a character in **minstrel shows**, which often featured white actors wearing dark makeup.

An elderly woman is about to break a law, drinking from a "white only" water fountain, as law enforcement officers look on.

WHITE ONLY

EDUCATION
and Character

Martin's interest in religion came from his father, but he was a bit unsure of his beliefs as a young man. King went to Booker T. Washington High School, where he skipped the ninth and twelfth grades. At age 15, he began to attend Morehouse College in Atlanta. He hoped to study either law or medicine at first, but finally decided to become a minister. King said that at Morehouse he saw religion could be *"intellectually respectful and emotionally satisfying."*

In his final year at Morehouse, King wrote about the nature of education in the school publication, *The Maroon Tiger: "We must remember that intelligence is not enough. Intelligence plus character—that is the goal of true education."* To King, true education should mold people of good character.

What King learned at Morehouse shaped the course of his ministry and life.

BUILDING CHARACTER

King credited the professors at Morehouse with greatly influencing his beliefs and later teachings. Morehouse president Dr. Benjamin E. Mays taught him about Mahatma Gandhi's nonviolent methods of protest against the British government in India. Professor Samuel W. Williams introduced him to Henry David Thoreau's "Essay on **Civil Disobedience**," which King read multiple times. King was fascinated by the idea of *"refusing to cooperate with an evil system."*

King graduated from Morehouse in 1948 with a degree in **sociology**. He became a minister at the age of 19 at Atlanta's Ebenezer Baptist Church in February 1948, and he received a Bachelor of Divinity degree from Crozer Theological Seminary in Chester, Pennsylvania, in 1951. That September, King began his doctoral studies at Boston University, completing them in 1955.

King moved to Montgomery, Alabama, to become the pastor of Dexter Avenue Baptist Church. The 5 years King spent at the Dexter Avenue church would be very active. He encouraged every member of the church to vote and to join the National Association for the Advancement of Colored People (NAACP), an organization that fights for the rights of blacks.

TAKING ACTION

King organized a "Social and Political Action Committee" within the Dexter Avenue Baptist Church. He wanted to make sure his church was informed about issues affecting their community and nation. King believed people should always be ready to speak out and defend their civil rights. *"The time is always right to do what's right,"* King later said. Two members of his church, Jo Ann Robinson and Rufus Lewis, were early organizers of the Montgomery bus **boycott**.

MORE TO KNOW

King's church is now a National Historic Landmark and is known as the Dexter Avenue King Memorial Baptist Church.

Martin Luther King Jr. was a powerful preacher. His manner of speaking made him an effective speaker in the civil rights movement, too.

The BUS BOYCOTT

On December 1, 1955, Rosa Parks—the secretary of the Montgomery chapter of the NAACP—refused a bus driver's order to give up her seat to a white man and move to the back of the bus. Parks was arrested and sent to jail. Leaders of the NAACP, including King and chapter president Edgar Nixon, decided it was time to fight bus segregation in Montgomery.

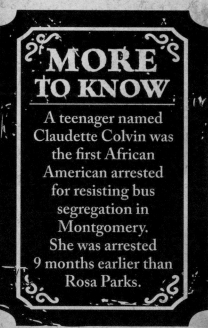

MORE TO KNOW

A teenager named Claudette Colvin was the first African American arrested for resisting bus segregation in Montgomery. She was arrested 9 months earlier than Rosa Parks.

King urged his church members to work to change their community for the better.

"We have no alternative but to protest," King said 4 days after Parks was arrested. "For many years we have shown an amazing patience . . . But we come here tonight to be saved from that patience that makes us patient with anything less than freedom and justice."

The newly formed Montgomery Improvement Association, led by King, made a boycott of the bus system their major goal.

Rosa Parks

In June 1956, a US court ruled racial segregation on buses was **unconstitutional** in the case *Browder v. Gayle*. The US Supreme Court upheld the decision in November. The Montgomery bus boycott ended in December 1956. King said, *"We came to see that, in the long run, it is more honorable to walk in dignity than ride in humiliation."* In 1957, King helped found the Southern Christian Leadership Conference (SCLC), of which he was elected president.

The Montgomery bus boycott wasn't without its dangers. King regularly received threats and was even arrested during the boycott. On January 30, 1956, the King family home was bombed. King was away organizing the boycott and no one was hurt, but it was a terrifying moment for King, his wife Coretta Scott King, and their first child, Yolanda.

King married Coretta Scott in 1953.

Civil rights leaders Ralph Abernathy (right) and W. J. Hudson inspect a home attacked in Montgomery, Alabama. King wasn't the only one in danger.

King met with an angry group of men looking for revenge on his behalf. Despite the bombing, he wouldn't allow violence in response to the attack. *"If you have weapons, take them home,"* he said. *"If you do not have them, please do not seek them. We cannot solve this problem through violence. We must meet violence with nonviolence."*

MORE TO KNOW

The Cleveland Avenue bus on which Rosa Parks refused to give up her seat is on display at the Henry Ford Museum in Dearborn, Michigan.

The Southern Christian Leadership Conference led more nonviolent protests, such as sit-ins at lunch counters where blacks weren't allowed to eat. Protestors would often be arrested, sprayed with fire hoses, or beaten by police officers, but King stressed the protestors should never answer with violence. He wanted blacks to obtain equal civil rights peacefully.

MORE TO KNOW

In 2010, it was revealed that King's friend and photographer Ernest Withers was an FBI informant.

"*The end of violence or the aftermath of violence is bitterness,*" he said in the speech "The Power of Nonviolence" from 1957. "*The aftermath of nonviolence is* **reconciliation** *and the creation of a beloved community. A boycott is never an end within itself. It is merely a means to awaken a sense of shame within the* **oppressor** *but the end is reconciliation, the end is* **redemption**." King believed that peaceful protest would bring forgiveness, togetherness, and understanding.

A sit-in is a nonviolent protest in which people occupy an area and refuse to leave until their demands have been met. This is a sit-in at a restaurant.

LUNCHEONETTE

THE FEDS ARE WATCHING

Despite King's nonviolent approach to the civil rights fight, many people thought he was dangerous. In late 1963, the Federal Bureau of Investigation (FBI) opened a file on King and closely followed the minister. They listened to his phone calls and had undercover agents watch him for signs of illegal activities. The FBI watched King closely until the day he died.

BEHIND
Bars

Even while under arrest and in jail, King tried to rally support for causes and make people aware of the civil rights movement. In his "Letter from Birmingham City Jail," King wrote, *"We must use time creatively, in the knowledge that the time is always ripe to do right."* King knew his cause couldn't wait for him to get out of jail, and his letter, written on April 16, 1963, proved to be a powerful tool in the fight for civil rights.

"Injustice anywhere is a threat to justice everywhere," he wrote in the letter, which was published in several magazines. King wrote as a response to some religious leaders who were critical of him and the other protestors. King and other civil rights leaders began to plan a massive rally.

PREPARED TO DIE

In the 1960s, the United States was a country of riots, protests, and sometimes violence. President John F. Kennedy was shot and killed in Dallas in 1963, and many say King expected more violence against himself as well. Speaking at a march in Detroit on June 23, 1963, King said that *"if a man has not discovered something that he will die for he isn't fit to live."*

Martin's actual signature:

Martin Luther King Jr.

Martin Luther King Jr. is fingerprinted by police after his arrest during the Montgomery bus boycott.

MORE TO KNOW

King was arrested 30 times during protests, speeches, and other demonstrations.

The DREAM

On August 28, 1963, King and other civil rights leaders held the March on Washington for Jobs and Freedom. More than 260,000 people gathered on the National Mall in Washington, DC, where King gave his most famous talk, known as the "I Have a Dream" speech. King spoke for 17 minutes in front of the massive crowd, as millions more watched on television:

MORE TO KNOW

An engraving honoring King's speech marks the spot where King spoke on the steps of the Lincoln Memorial.

I have a dream that one day this nation will rise up, live out the true meaning of its creed: 'We hold these truths to be self-evident, that all men are created equal.'. . . I have a dream that my four little children will one day live in a nation where they will not be judged by the color of their skin but by the content of their character.

FREE AT LAST

King called for freedom everywhere, from the *"hilltops of New Hampshire"* to the *"Rockies of Colorado"* to the *"slopes of California."* *"Let freedom ring from Stone Mountain of Georgia,"* he cried. The speech ended with King referring to a song once sung by slaves, *"and when we allow freedom to ring, . . . [we] will be able to join hands and sing in the words of the old Negro spiritual, 'Free at last, Free at last, Thank God A-mighty, We are free at last!'"*

King quoted the Declaration of Independence in his speech. The Declaration's promise of freedom didn't ring true for blacks at that time.

NOBEL PRIZE

PEACE SPEAKER

As the Vietnam War (1954–1975) intensified, King increasingly called for an end to the conflict in speeches and sermons. *"As I have walked among the desperate, rejected, and angry young men, I have told them that Molotov cocktails and rifles will not solve their problems,"* he said in an April 1967 sermon. *"But they ask, and rightfully so, 'What about Vietnam?'"* King said he couldn't stand by while his government used violence to solve its problems.

In 1964, Martin Luther King Jr. won the Nobel Peace Prize. He received the award in Oslo, Norway, and began his speech by saying, *"I accept the Nobel Prize for Peace at a moment when 22 million negroes of the United States of America are engaged in a creative battle to end the long night of racial injustice."*

Dedicating the award to the civil rights movement, King spoke of the resolve his fellow activists felt after the March on Washington: *"I accept this award today with an abiding faith in America and an **audacious** faith in the future of mankind."* He promised he would *"refuse to accept despair"* and that he'd keep hoping and working for change.

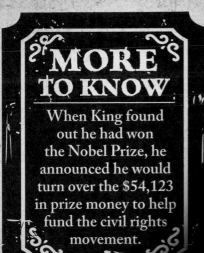

MORE TO KNOW

When King found out he had won the Nobel Prize, he announced he would turn over the $54,123 in prize money to help fund the civil rights movement.

At age 35, Martin Luther King Jr. was the youngest person to ever win the Nobel Peace Prize.

FREE
at Last

MORE TO KNOW

King marched three times on the Alabama state capitol in 1965, finally reaching the building on the third march.

After years of protesting, countless speeches, and the efforts of millions, President Lyndon Johnson signed the Civil Rights Act of 1964 into law. The landmark legislation outlawed segregation in public places, including schools and restaurants, as well as discrimination in the workplace. In 1965, Johnson signed into law the Voting Rights Act, which aimed to end laws that kept people from voting.

"They told us we wouldn't get here," King said in a 1965 speech. *"And there were those who said that we would get here only over their dead bodies. But all the world today knows that we are here and we are standing before the forces of power in the state of Alabama saying, 'We ain't goin' let nobody turn us around.'"*

STILL FIGHTING

Many states were slow to adopt the civil rights measures. King continued to march for rights in states such as Alabama, where protestors were met with police violence.

He urged his followers to continue fighting with confidence. *"I've seen the promised land,"* King said in 1965. *"I may not get there with you. But I want you to know tonight, that we, as a people, will get to the promised land."*

King stands behind President Johnson as he signs the Civil Rights Act into law in 1964.

MOUNTAIN
of Despair

WE REMEMBER

In 1983, Martin Luther King Jr. Day became a national holiday. Every third Monday in January is set aside to remember King's legacy of peace and the fight for civil rights in the United States. The Lorraine Motel was converted into the National Civil Rights Museum in 1991. The motel and its balcony remain unchanged, with a wreath hanging where King was killed outside room 306. The motel's sign still stands today.

In April 1968, King visited Memphis, Tennessee, to give support to protesting **sanitation workers**. At 6:01 p.m. on April 4, King was standing on a balcony at the Lorraine Motel when he was fatally shot. He died an hour later. King was 39. A man named James Earl Ray was arrested for the crime 2 months later.

President Johnson called for a national day of mourning on April 7. King's funeral was held on April 9, and thousands of people attended the two services held in Atlanta, Georgia. King's body was laid to rest in South View Cemetery until his remains were moved in 1977 to what is now the Martin Luther King Jr. National Historic Site.

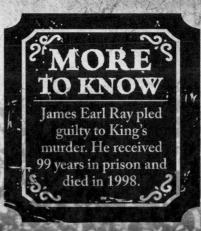

The casket of civil rights leader Dr. Martin Luther King Jr. is carried through Atlanta streets by a mule-drawn wagon.

MORE TO KNOW

James Earl Ray pled guilty to King's murder. He received 99 years in prison and died in 1998.

STONE
of Hope

MORE TO KNOW

The memorial's address is 1964 Independence Avenue, a nod to the landmark 1964 Civil Rights Act passed with King's help.

"This is our hope," King said during his "I Have a Dream" speech. *"This is the faith that I go back to the South with. With this faith we will be able to* **hew** *out of the mountain of despair a stone of hope."*

On August 28, 2011—48 years after King's most famous speech—the Martin Luther King Jr. Memorial opened on the National Mall in Washington, DC. Out of tons of white granite rises a 30-foot (9.1 m) sculpture of the civil rights icon who helped so many gain the rights promised to them almost a century earlier. While Stone Mountain reminded King of slavery and oppression during his lifetime, his own stone reminds all Americans of the power of hope and nonviolence.

TIMELINE
THE LIFE OF
MARTIN LUTHER KING JR.

Martin Luther King Jr. is born Michael King Jr. on January 15 — **1929**

1934 — King's name is changed to Martin Luther King Jr.

Martin attends Morehouse College at age 15 — **1944**

1948 — King graduates from Morehouse with a degree in sociology

King becomes pastor at Dexter Avenue Baptist Church in Montgomery, Alabama — **1954**

1955 — Martin Luther King Jr. is a leader of the Montgomery bus boycott

King delivers the "I Have a Dream" speech in Washington, DC — **1963**

1964 — The Civil Rights Act is passed

King is the youngest person ever to win the Nobel Peace Prize

The Voting Rights Act is passed — **1965**

1968 — King is shot in Memphis, Tennessee, on April 4

Martin Luther King Jr. Memorial opens in Washington, DC — **2011**

GLOSSARY

audacious: bold, daring, or fearless

boycott: the act of refusing to have dealings with a person or business in order to force change

civil disobedience: the breaking of a law as a form of nonviolent protest to force change

Confederate: having to do with the Confederate States of America (the Southern states) during the American Civil War

hew: to cut or carve something from stone or wood

minstrel show: a performance in which an actor wears blackface makeup while singing and dancing

Molotov cocktail: a bomb made of a bottle and flammable liquid that is lit and then thrown

oppressor: one who acts harshly or cruelly to keep others from gaining power

reconciliation: the ending of a conflict

redemption: the saving or improving of something in a poor state

sanitation worker: one who hauls trash away from people's houses

segregation: the forced separation of races or classes

sociology: the study of the origin, development, and structure of societies and the behavior of individuals and groups

unconstitutional: describing something that goes against the US Constitution

FOR MORE
Information

Books

Aretha, David. *Martin Luther King Jr. and the 1963 March on Washington*. Greensboro, NC: Morgan Reynolds Publishing, 2014.

Ganeri, Anita. *I Have a Dream: Martin Luther King Jr. and the Fight for Equal Rights*. Mankato, MN: Smart Apple Media, 2013.

Herrington, Lisa M. *Martin Luther King Jr. Day*. New York, NY: Children's Press, 2013.

Websites

I Have a Dream
www.thekingcenter.org/archive/document/i-have-dream-1
Read the full text of Martin Luther King Jr.'s famous speech, and check out more about the Martin Luther King Jr. Center for Nonviolent Social Change.

Martin Luther King Jr.
nobelprize.org/nobel_prizes/peace/laureates/1964/king-bio.html
Read more about Martin Luther King Jr.'s accomplishments on this site.

Martin Luther King Jr. Day of Service
mlkday.gov
Find out how you can help others on the official Martin Luther King Jr. Day of Service site.

INDEX